WHAT MATTERS MOST?

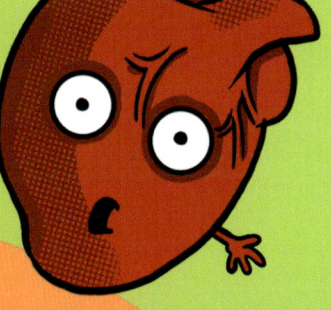

HUMAN BODY BITS

Paul Mason
Nigel Baines

WAYLAND

First published in Great Britain in 2024
by Wayland

Copyright © Hodder and Stoughton, 2024

All rights reserved

Editor: Sarah Peutrill
Designer: Nigel Baines
Science consultant: Peter Riley

ISBN (HB): 978 1 5263 2421 4
ISBN (PB): 978 1 5263 2422 1

Printed and bound in Dubai

Wayland, an imprint of
Hachette Children's Group
Part of Hodder and Stoughton
Carmelite House
50 Victoria Embankment
London EC4Y 0DZ

An Hachette UK Company
www.hachette.co.uk
www.hachettechildrens.co.uk

FSC
www.fsc.org
MIX
Paper from
responsible sources
FSC® C104740

Contents

Which body bit matters most?   4
Brain: Mission control   6
Eyes, ears and nose: Sense organs   8
Nervous system: Sending messages   10
Mouth: The body's gateway   12
Lungs (and diaphragm): Breathing   14
Heart: Always pumping   16
Red blood cells: The body's busiest bits   16
White blood cells: Fighting for you   18
Digestive system: Team Intestine!   20
Skeleton and muscles: Heavy lifting   24
Skin: Keeping it all in (and out!)   26
The winner is …   28
Glossary   29
Body systems   30
Index   32

Which body bit matters most?

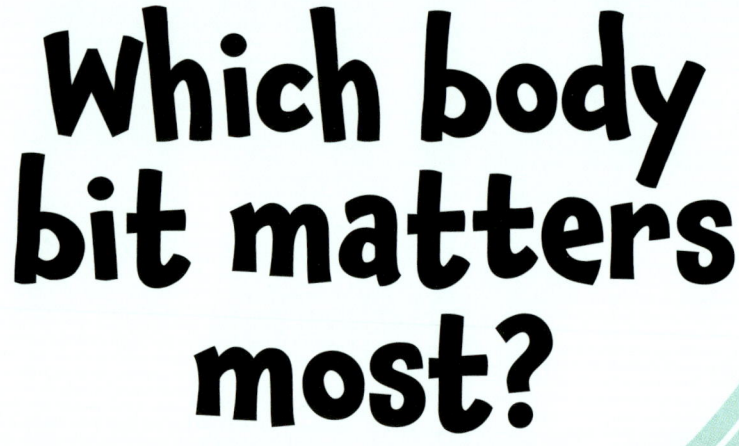

I'm a cell. I may look simple – but even the most complicated bits of your body are made up of cells like me.

In total you are made of about 37 trillion cells.

37,000,000,000,000

Different kinds of cell make up ...

I wish people wouldn't walk all over me.

... your bones

Without bones, you'd just be a blob of human on the floor.

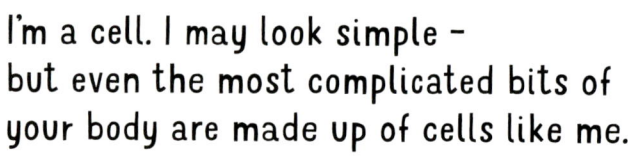

... your skin

You definitely need skin. It keeps your insides inside you.

Hey, you dropped your insides all over my new clean floor!

... your brain

Without a brain, you wouldn't be able to do ANYTHING.

Although, being able to do things and having a brain sometimes don't seem to go together!

... and every other body bit

Some body bits are more important than others – but which is MOST important? Let's ask some body bits and see what they say.

I'm the most important.

I think you'll find it's me.

Oh dear, I don't think so.

Surely, it's me?

No, No, NO!

Brain
Mission control

PAY ATTENTION! I'm in charge here. And this OBVIOUSLY makes me the most important.

People say I'm bossy – but without me the others wouldn't know what to do.
Just look at all the jobs I do ...

My important bits are cells called neurons. They do the thinking.

Do you think people could survive without us neurons?

Don't even think about it.

Eyes, ears and nose
Sense organs

Brain might THINK it's important – but where does Brain get its information? Us, that's where!

Without us, you wouldn't know what was going on around you.

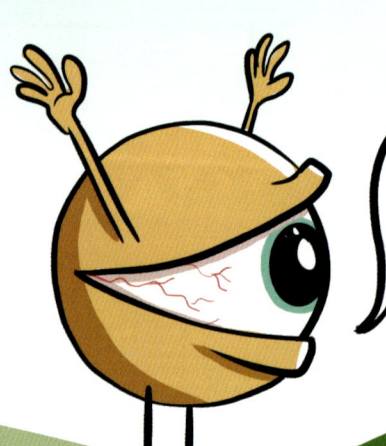

Just think about all the things I do for you.

I help you read this book, see tiny things close up and big things like that cow a long way away.

MOOOO

Here's what happened ...

"Should have worn shoes."

"We've decoded the message from the toe, boss. It says, 'OW!'"

The pain receptor releases a message. It passes along a nerve and up your spine. Fractions of a second later ... Aargh!

Special cells in your toe, called pain receptors, turn on.

"Ouch! That will be painful. Better send a message to the brain."

Mouth
The body's gateway

I'm the gateway into your body for three things that keep you alive: air, water and food.

Mouth forgets that I help you to bring in air too!

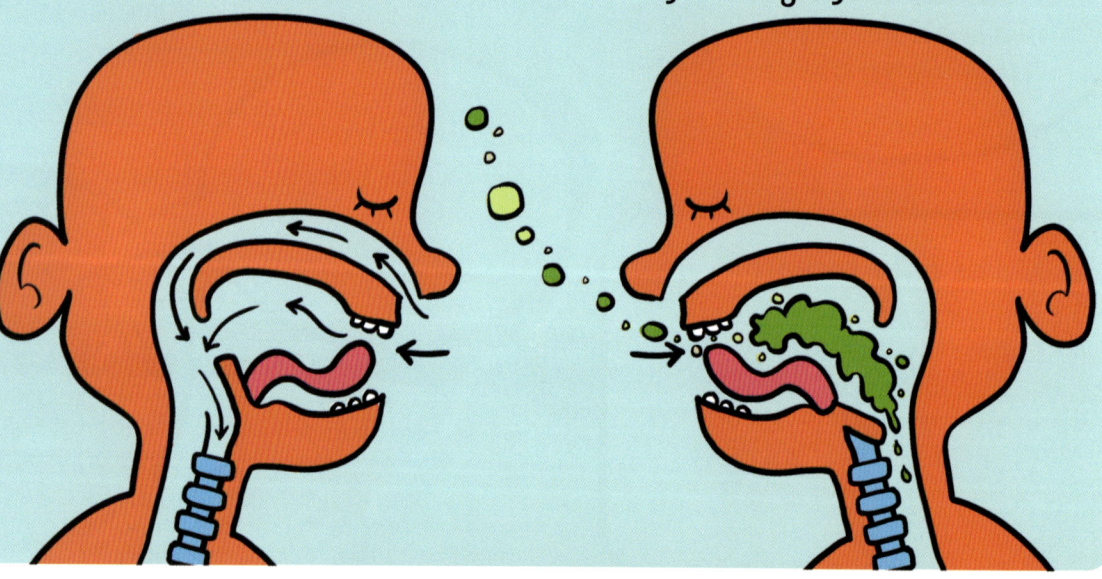

Air is pulled into your mouth.

Food and water go into your body through your mouth.

Lungs (and Diaphragm)
Breathing

No one can live without oxygen – which gets into your body through us, your lungs.

Look how hard we (and your diaphragm) work for you all the time.

When you need a breath ... your diaphragm pulls down on us. At the same time, the muscles around us relax. Air is sucked in.

Sniff

I'm just a LITTLE bit bigger than my friend over there ...

Diaphragm here. I seem to do most of the work!

Next I move the oxygen from the air into your blood. Now the oxygen can be transported around your body to where it is needed.

While we're at it, we take out the trash. Your body makes a poisonous gas called carbon dioxide. Your blood drops it off with us.

What did we do wrong?

Diaphragm relaxes and the muscles around us tighten up. We get smaller and everything whooshes out.

Shut UP! You know I have to make space for the heart!

WHOOSH!

So, us lungs deliver life-giving oxygen into your body, and remove a deadly poisonous gas. We MUST be the body bit that matters most?

... and relax.

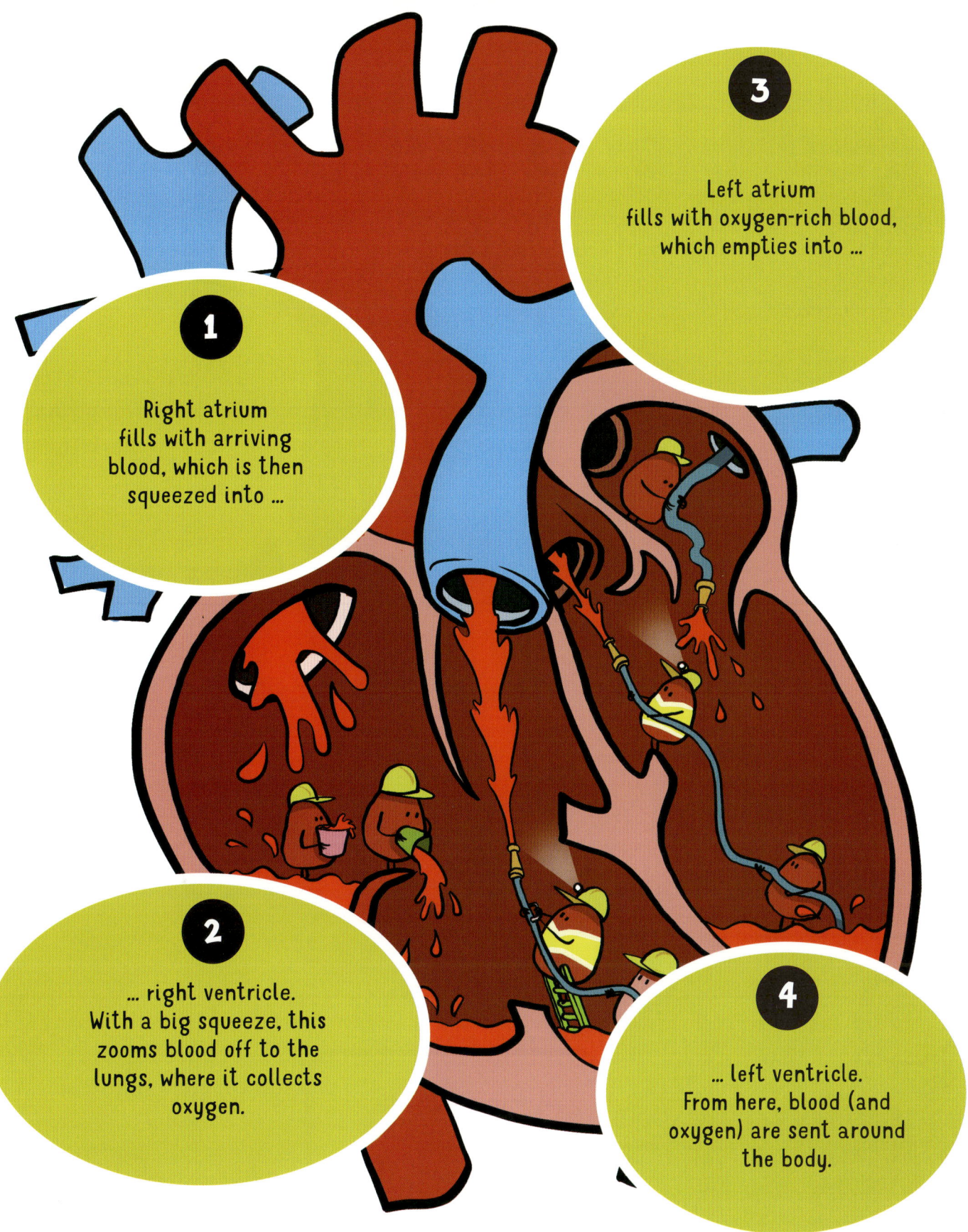

Red blood cells
The body's busiest bits

"Look, I can't stop. My friends and I have a LOT of work to do."

We leave the heart and race along an artery (a highway for blood) to the lungs.

"Wee-hee!"

"Hey, stop pushing!"

"Phew!"

At the lungs, we collect as much oxygen as we can carry, then head straight back to the heart. There's no time to lose!

Oxygen makes us go bright red.

Blush

White blood cells
Fighting for you!

We've got a virus coming in to sector twelve.

Us white blood cells are your body's defence force. We fight diseases and infections that attack you.

We fight in different ways depending on who's attacking and how.

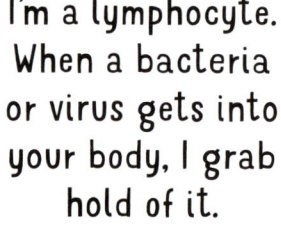

I'm a lymphocyte. When a bacteria or virus gets into your body, I grab hold of it.

Oi!

Next I produce a chemical called an antibody. The antibody destroys the invader.

I'm a phagocyte. I grab invaders, surround them, and then ...

Uh oh!

... I pretty much eat it. I also store a little reminder, for next time I meet an invader like this one.

 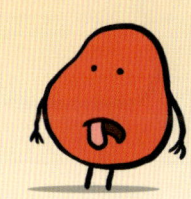

Yuck, that's disgusting!

Surely fighting off deadly invaders such as viruses means we REALLY matter?

Digestive system
Team Intestine!

Your body can't run without fuel – and we at Team Intestine feed you the fuel.

Once you have swallowed your food through your mouth, it reaches me – your stomach.

I mix it with acid, then churn it all up until it becomes a liquid called chyme.

CHURN! CHURN!

The chyme is released into me, your small intestine.

Skeleton and muscles
Heavy lifting

You know how you just turned the page of this book? You couldn't do it without us!

Look at all the work that goes into just holding the paper ...

First, the bones in your hand give it shape.

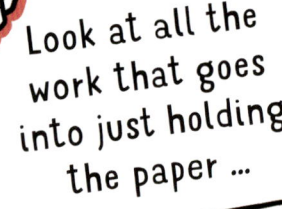

Bones cannot move without muscles to help them. Skeleton and muscles usually work as a team.

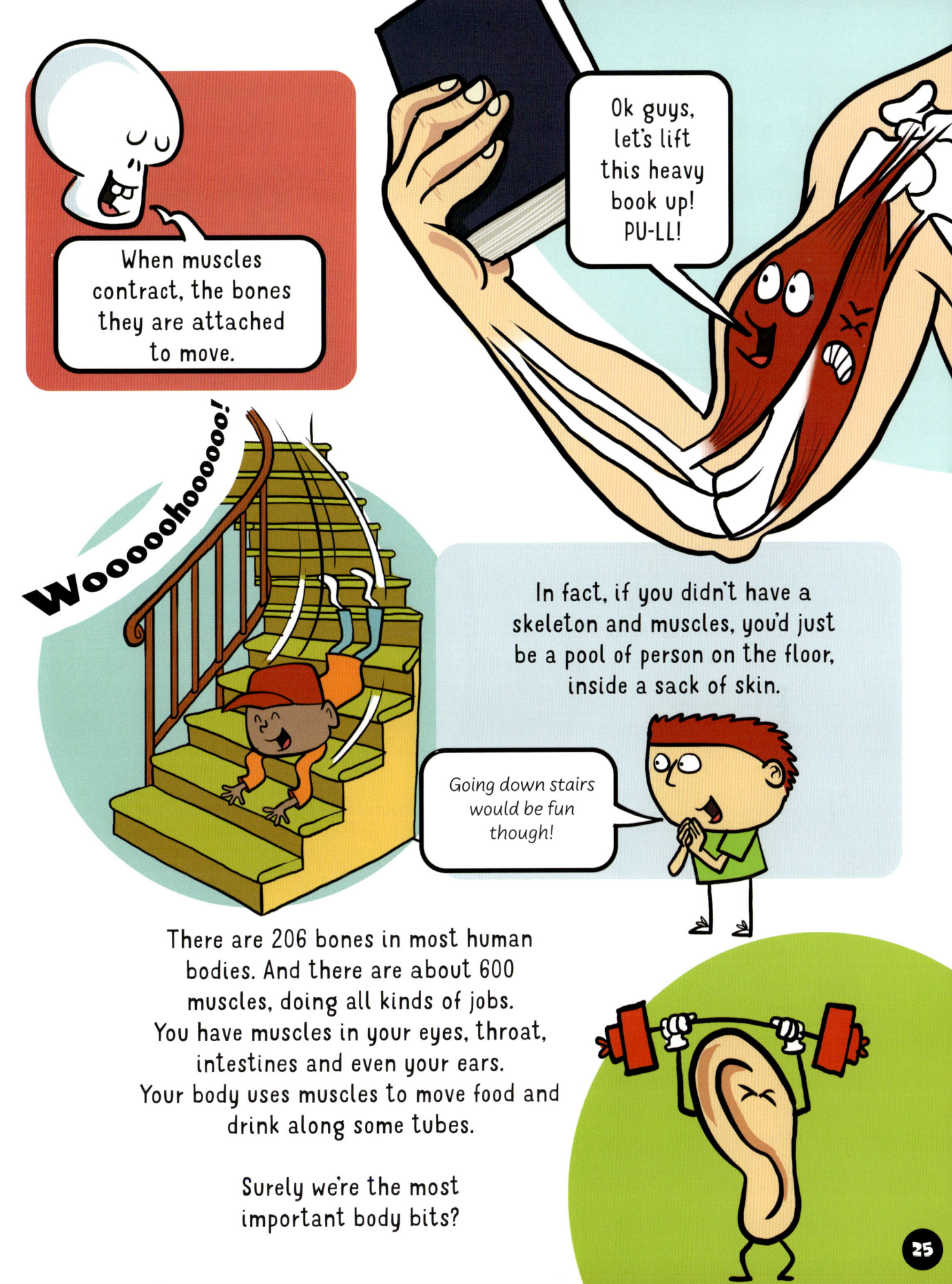

Skin
Keeping it all in (and out!)

Her hair is perfect for sledding!!

Keeping your insides inside you is my biggest job – but I have lots of others.

I'm made up of three main layers. From outside to inside, they are the epidermis, the dermis and the hypodermis*.

Each layer has lots of different jobs. So many, actually, that I've only got space to tell you about the main ones.

* Dermis means 'skin' in ancient Greek, in case you were wondering.

Hair

Epidermis

Dermis

Hypodermis

The winner is ...
Does there have to be a winner?

ALL your body bits have to work together, to keep you as well as possible. For example ...

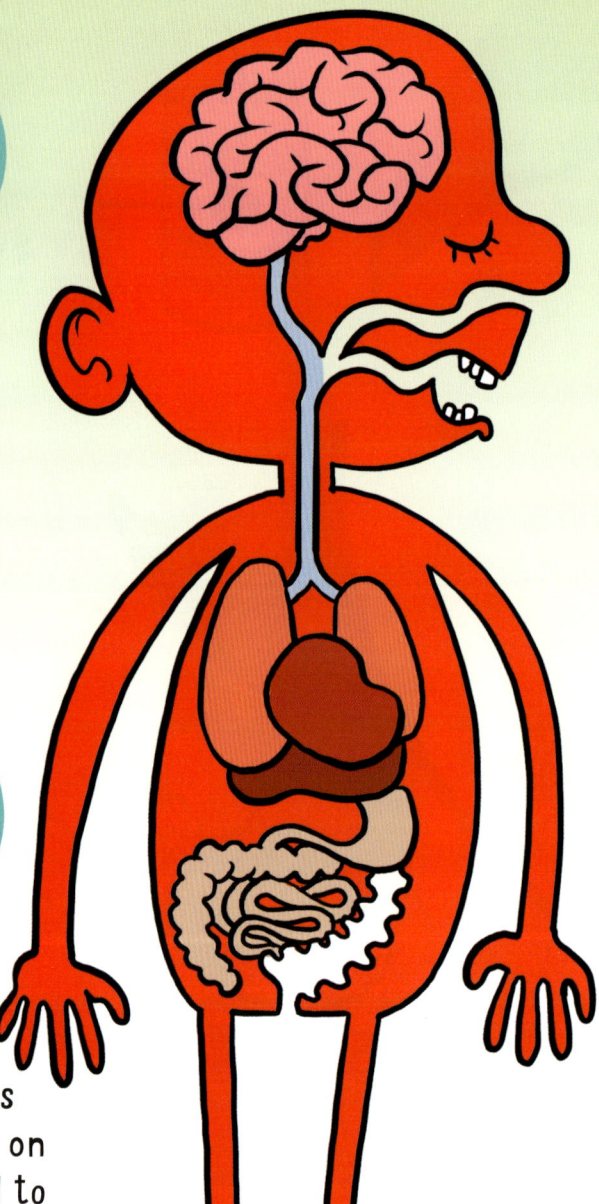

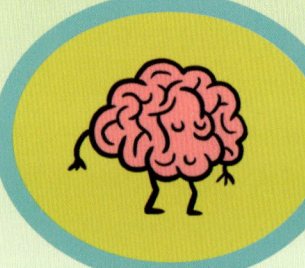

The brain controls everything – but without bony protection, and blood, it couldn't survive.

Your heart and blood need your lungs – otherwise they wouldn't have any oxygen to deliver.

Muscles and bones need nutrients from food. They rely on intestines and blood to deliver this.

Glossary

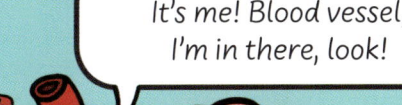

It's me! Blood vessel, I'm in there, look!

blood vessel
a narrow tube that carries blood

carbon dioxide
a gas that is produced when some things are burned, and also when humans and other animals breathe out

cell
the smallest unit of something living

contract
get smaller or squeeze together

diaphragm
a curved sheet of muscle attached to the bottom of the lungs

infection
something that causes your body illness or disease

intestines
organs in the body that break down food so it can be used for energy

organ
a part of your body that has a particular job. For example, your heart's job is to pump blood around your body

oxygen
a gas that humans breathe in, then use to make energy in their muscles

nutrient
something a living thing needs to survive and grow

receptor
a cell that reacts to, for example, heat or light by sending a signal through the nervous system

sense
the ability to perceive see, hear, smell, taste and/or touch (these are the five 'senses')

Body systems

The body bits that introduced themselves in this book are all part of different body systems. A system is a group of things that work together.

Brain and nervous system

Your brain and nervous system work together. The nervous system carries messages around your body. Most of these messages go to or from the brain. The brain is also where your memories are stored and the place where thinking happens.

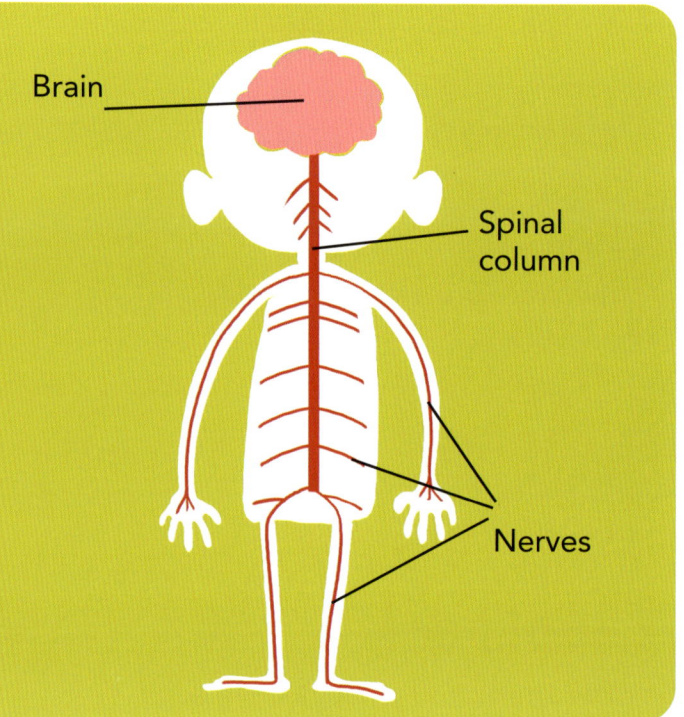

Digestive system

This starts at your mouth and finishes at your bottom. It is one long tube that runs all the way through you. In some places – such as your stomach – the tube is wider. As food and drink pass through, the digestive system removes the things your body needs.

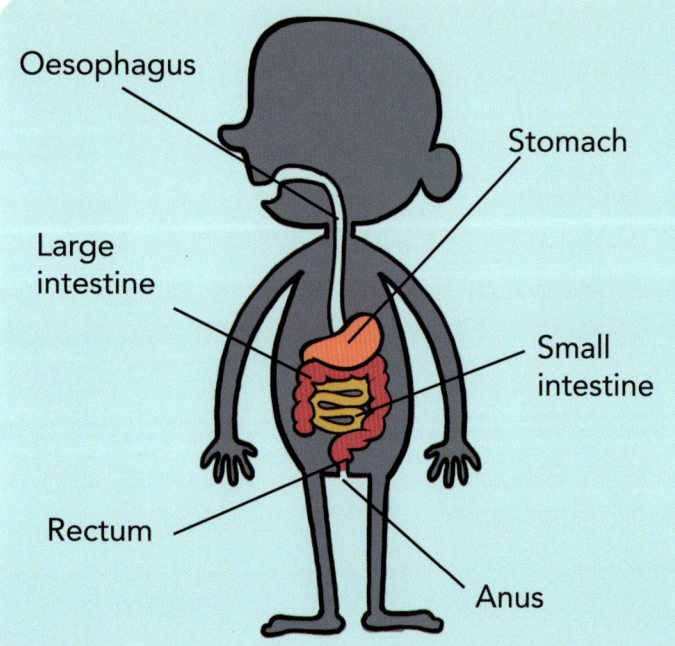

Respiratory system

The respiratory system is the network of body bits that helps you breathe. This happens in your lungs. Here oxygen is taken in and carbon dioxide is released in tiny pockets called alveoli. The gases arrive and leave along your windpipe, or trachea.

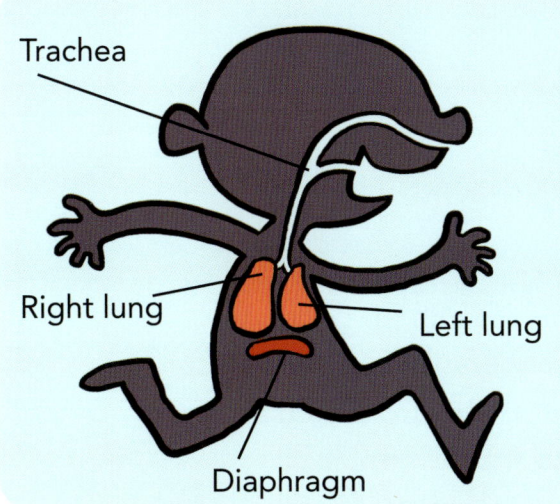

Skeleton and muscular system

The skeleton and muscular system work together to give your body shape (the skeleton's job) and let it move (which your muscles help with). Muscles that help you move are called 'skeletal muscles'.

Other muscles inside your body have different jobs. For example, the muscles in your digestive system squeeze and widen to move food along.

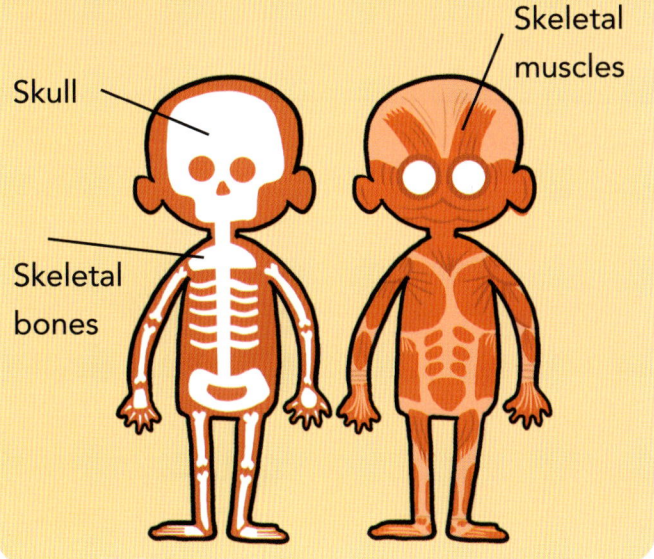

Circulatory system

This carries blood around your body. Blood is one of your body's main delivery services, taking food and oxygen to where it is needed and collecting waste. Blood also contains white blood cells (which are actually colourless, not white) that defend you against disease and infection. The circulatory system is powered by your heart.

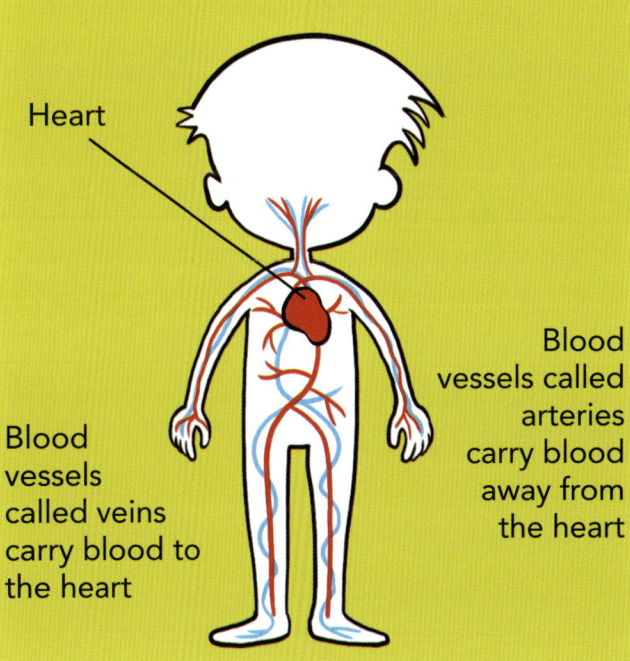

Index

blood 15, 17-21, 23, 28
    antibodies 21
    lymphocytes 20
    phagocytes 21
    red blood cells 18-19
    white blood cells 20-21
blood vessels 18-19
    arteries 18-19
    capillaries 19
bones 4, 24-25, 28
brain 5-8, 10-11, 28
breathing 7, 12-15

carbon dioxide 15, 19
cells 4, 6, 11, 27
    blood cells 18-21
neurons 6

diaphragm 14-15
digestive system 12-13, 22-23

ears 8-9, 25
eating 7, 12-13
eyes 8-9, 25

germs 20-21, 27
    bacteria 20
    viruses 20-21

hair 26-27
heart 15-19, 28

immune system
    (defence against germs) 20-21
intestines 22-23, 25, 28
    large intestine 23, 25
    small intestine 22, 25

lungs 14-15, 17-19, 28

mouth 12-13, 22
movement 7, 14-15, 24-25
muscles 14-15, 24-25, 28

nervous system/nerves 10-11
nose 8-9
nutrients 23, 28

oxygen 14-15, 17-19, 28

poo 23

senses 7-10
skeleton 24-25
skin 5, 25-27
stomach 22

teeth 13

I'll wave goodbye now ...